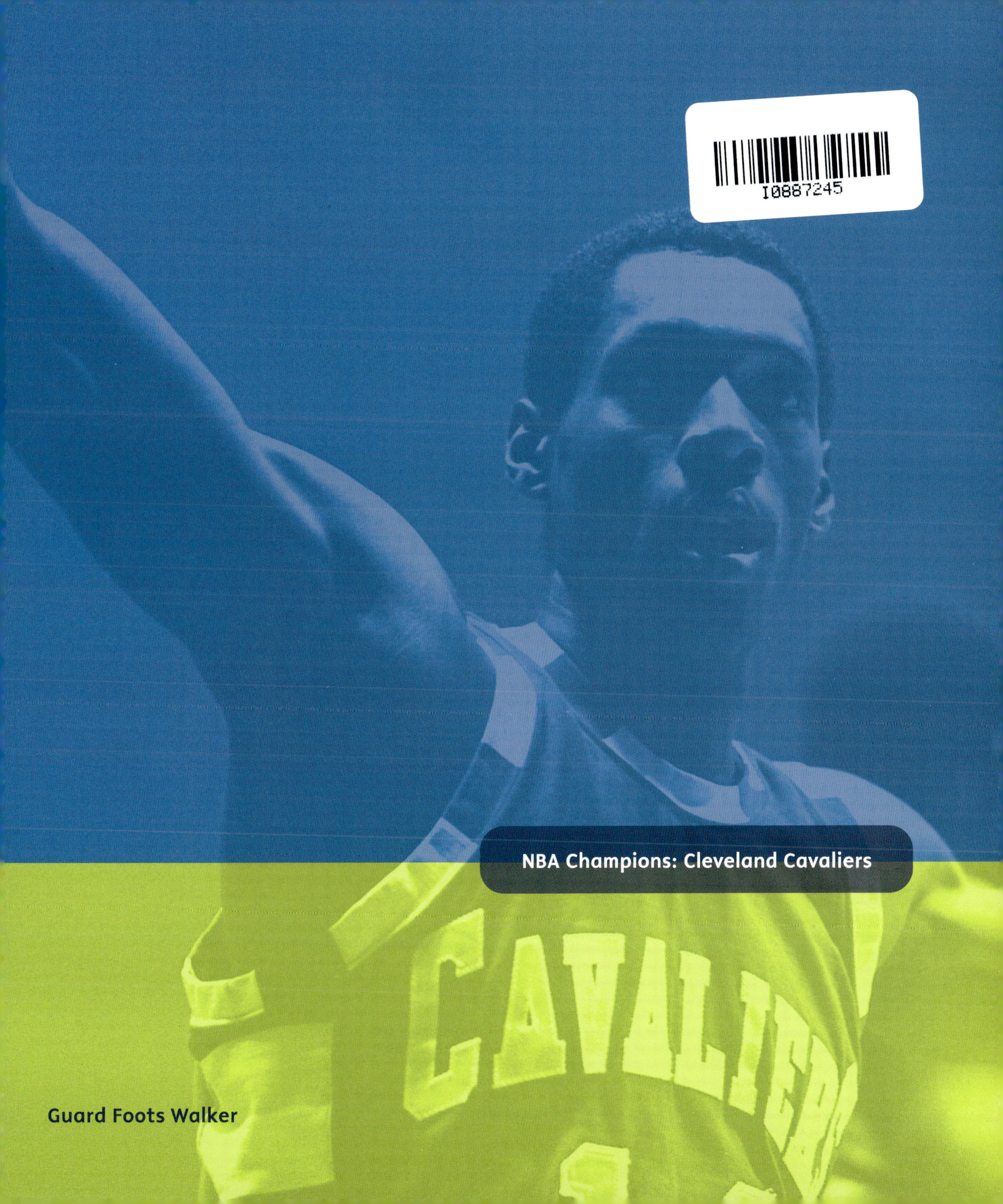

NBA Champions: Cleveland Cavaliers

Guard Foots Walker

Forward LeBron James

NBA CHAMPIONS

CLEVELAND CAVALIERS

BY JOE TISCHLER

CREATIVE SPORTS

CREATIVE EDUCATION / CREATIVE PAPERBACKS

Guard Ron Harper

Published by Creative Education and Creative Paperbacks
P.O. Box 227, Mankato, Minnesota 56002
Creative Education and Creative Paperbacks are imprints of
The Creative Company
www.thecreativecompany.us

Art Direction by Tom Morgan
Book production by Graham Morgan
Edited by Grace Cain

Images by Getty Images/Carmen Mandato, 10, Charlotte Observer, 16, David Liam Kyle, 19, Dick Raphael, 4, 7, Focus On Sport, 12, 15, Gregory Shamus, cover, Justin Ford, 20, Kevin Cooley, 9, Manny Millan, 5, Mark Blinch, 3, Nathaniel S. Butler, 2, Rogers Photo Archive, 1, Tony Tomsic, 24; Newscom/David Maxwell, cover; US Presswire/David Butler II, 6

Library of Congress Cataloging-in-Publication Data
Names: Tischler, Joe, author.
Title: Cleveland Cavaliers / by Joe Tischler.
Description: Mankato, Minnesota : Creative Education and Creative Paperbacks, 2025. | Series: Creative sports: NBA champions | Includes index. | Audience: Ages 7-10 | Audience: Grades 2-3 | Summary: "Elementary-level text and dynamic sports photos highlight the NBA championship win of the Cleveland Cavaliers, plus sensational players associated with the professional basketball team such as Donovan Mitchell"— Provided by publisher.
Identifiers: LCCN 2024014042 (print) | LCCN 2024014043 (ebook) | ISBN 9798889892526 (library binding) | ISBN 9781682776186 (paperback) | ISBN 9798889893639 (ebook)
Subjects: LCSH: Cleveland Cavaliers (Basketball team)—History—Juvenile literature. | Basketball players—United States—Juvenile literature.
Classification: LCC GV885.52.C57 T57 2025 (print) | LCC GV885.52.C57 (ebook) | DDC 796.3230977132—dc23/eng/20240405
LC record available at https://lccn.loc.gov/2024014042
LC ebook record available at https://lccn.loc.gov/2024014043

Printed in China

Center Brad Daugherty

Guard Mo Williams

CONTENTS

Home of the Cavaliers

Cleveland is a large city in Ohio. It sits along the shores of Lake Erie. That's one of the Great Lakes. The Rock and Roll Hall of Fame is there. The city is also home to an **arena** called Rocket Mortgage FieldHouse. It's home to a basketball team called the Cavaliers.

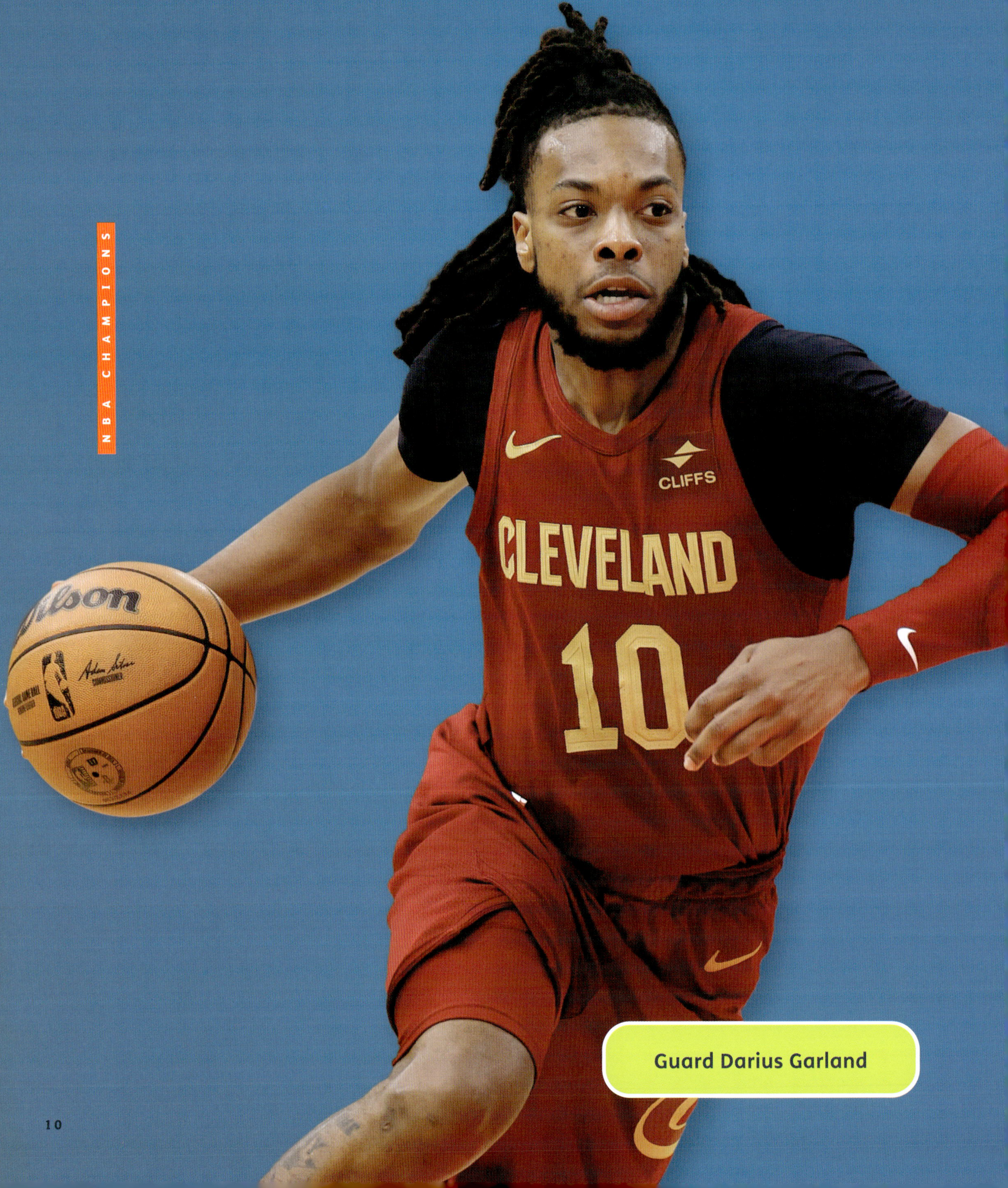

Guard Darius Garland

The Cleveland Cavaliers are a National Basketball Association (NBA) team. They play in the Central Division. That's part of the Eastern Conference. Their **rivals** are the Chicago Bulls and Detroit Pistons. All NBA teams want to win the NBA Finals and become champions.

Guard Austin Carr

Naming the Cavaliers

Fans voted on the team name. The poll was conducted by a Cleveland newspaper. Cavaliers was chosen from a list of five finalists. The person who submitted the name said, "Cavaliers represent a group of daring, fearless men."

Cavaliers History

The Cavaliers began play in 1970. They were not very good at first. They made the playoffs for the first time in 1976. They reached the conference finals. Jim Chones scored the most points and blocked the most shots. Jim Brewer played defense and led in **rebounds**.

Lenny Wilkens became head coach in 1986. Cleveland became consistent winners. Mark Price dished out a lot of **assists**. They reached the conference finals again in 1992. They lost to Michael Jordan and the Chicago Bulls.

Center Jim Chones

Forward LeBron James

Cleveland found gold in the 2003 NBA Draft. They selected Ohio native LeBron James with the first pick. His nickname was "The Chosen One." The Cavaliers made their first NBA Finals in 2007. But they lost to the San Antonio Spurs. James added two **Most Valuable Player (MVP)** awards. He left the team.

James came back in 2015. Cleveland made four straight NBA Finals. They won the Finals in 2016. They beat the Golden State Warriors in seven games. It was their first championship! James stopped a key score with a block at the end of Game 7. Kyrie Irving hit a big shot to seal the win.

Other Cavaliers Stars

The Cavaliers have had many other great stars. Larry Nance was a great defender. He was also known for his slam dunks. He was teammates with Brad Daugherty. Daugherty played in five All-Star Games.

Kevin Love played nine seasons with Cleveland. He played in two All-Star Games. He was on the 2016 **title** team. So was Tristan Thompson. He played nine seasons with the team.

Forward Larry Nance

Guard Donovan Mitchell

Donovan Mitchell and Darius Garland are great scorers on the team today. Cavaliers fans hope they can help bring another championship to Cleveland soon!

About the Cavaliers

First season: 1970–71

Conference/division: Eastern Conference, Central Division

Team colors: wine, gold, and black

Home arena: Rocket Mortgage FieldHouse

NBA CHAMPIONSHIPS:

2016, 4 games to 3 over Golden State Warriors

TEAM WEBSITE:

https://www.nba.com/cavaliers/

Glossary

arena—a large building with seats for spectators, where sports games and entertainment events are held

assist—a basketball pass that leads to a basket

Most Valuable Player (MVP)—an honor given to the season's best player

rebound—getting the ball after a missed shot

rival—a team that plays extra hard against another team

title—another word for championship

1970s Cleveland Cavaliers

Index